Liberia in the Colorful World of Diplomacy

John S. M. Yormie Jr.

Forte Publishing

First Published in 2019
Published by:

FORTE Publications
#12 Ashmun Street
Snapper Hill
Monrovia, Liberia
[+231] 88-110-6177

FORTE Publishing
7202 Tavenner Lane
208 Alexandria
VA, 22306

FORTE Press
76 Sarasit Road
Ban Pong, 70110
Ratchaburi, Thailand
[+66] 85-824-4382

http//:fortepublishing.wix.com/fppp
fortepublishing@gmail.com

Printed in the United States of America.

ISBN-13: 978-0-6481823-9-9

Dedication

I find myself in a priceless world of care, having superb glamour of parental adoration; an enviable circle of supportive friends whom I am pleased to collectively dedicate this book.

Table of Contents

Foreword

Liberia, a nation born out of the forging of peoples of African descent, including those who returned from the United States and indigenous groups that they met, has a very rich and unique history. After gaining its independence in 1847, Liberia was in the vanguard in the struggle for the independence of colonized African countries. In this way, Liberia has been a forerunner of African liberation and self-determination.

As a founding member of the Organization of African Unity (now African Union), the United Nations and its specialized agencies, and the Non-Aligned Movement, Liberia remains a firm believer in the usefulness of these organizations and in their sacred principles of global humanity, human dignity and respectability.

In this spirit, John Yormie has pieced together short articles, opinion pieces, and poems in his book entitled "Liberia in the Colorful World of Diplomacy", to recount this small nation's (Liberia) importance in sub-regional, regional and global politics. The articles, which are focused on historical, political and socio-economic realities of Liberia, consider both the early stages of Liberia as a nation and its roles in the struggle for an independent Africa. Since a comprehensive synthesis of Liberian history has yet to be written, any intrepid author, who attempts this task, must surely make extensive use of John Yorimie's Liberia in Colorful World of Diplomacy,

Augustine Konneh (PhD)
Dean of Graduate School
A.M.E. University

Acknowledgement

Much is owed to many who have inspired my sojourn and I herein find it a pleasure to acknowledge those who have most recently shaped my thinking and encouraged me to write short pieces, which I have compiled in this book.

I want to begin with Professor Robert Llyod of the Pepperdine University, USA, who was a visiting Professor at the Jindal School of International Affairs, Jindal Global University, India; thanks to Professor Rajdeep Pakanati, who supervised my MA Dissertation and inspired me to research and analyze large data. Mr. Cewhy Kwanue of the Daily Observer Newspaper, Liberia, who boosted my desire to publish on myriad societal issues, much appreciation.

Most particularly, so much is owed to Rev. J. Emmanuel Bowier, who guided me in identifying relevant topics and book sources along with D. Othniel Forte, who significantly provided editorial services for the completion of this book.

Introduction

For a long time, my desire has been to write. Issues close to my heart solicited a need to write about them. My interest and practice evolved from writing term papers, short articles, to research dissertations, and now a book.

The collection of some of these short articles and poems resulted in this book. When compiling the chapters, a key concern was to include articles that could each be studied as standalones, yet, not lose the collective theme. I believe we achieved this goal.

Mostly, the chapters herein focus on the historical, socio-political, economic realities of Liberia. They consider both early stages of the Liberian nation-state and its roles in the fight for an independent Africa. The book is an introductory text, much of the details are in the next book. One should hold this important consideration throughout the chapters. It will clear up most questions on why the author omitted and/or did not discuss them in depth.

As one reads this book, it will help to note the following.

Chapter One briefly covers the critical role Liberia played in international diplomacy. It offers reasons for the fading legacy. Being an introduction, several critical roles, were omitted, however, they will be in the next book.

Chapter Two takes on the issue of cultural diplomacy and how it can be used to further national policy, if done properly.

Chapter Three discusses human security both domestically and internationally. It talks about how Liberia can design policies and situate itself to benefit from it.

Chapter Four makes a case for a rethink on national politics and policy. It draws a case from the past and links it to current realities.

Chapter Five takes two cases of bureaucratic reform, which recently occurred. It argues for a replication of these success stories.

Chapter Six makes a case for a stronger Corporate Social Responsibility (CSR) as a part of a national development plan.

Chapter Seven tackles the climate change issue as a potential crisis breeding ground.

The Patriots' Creed

Behold the flows of Kpatawee waterfall
a source of survival as a people.
Surrounded by neighbors, all different,
yet we coexist peacefully and the Atlantic Ocean
the first witness o'er which the Lone Star flew
and showed Africa's first hope

Mount Nimba, defiant, majestic, is the peak
upon which we stood tall to provide economic
and political relief for the entire Africa

Our civil war, a *not so pretty*, low point but a
testament to our desire to remain a united,
undivided people

Liberia, an ever-beating heart;
Liberia, an evidence of resilience
Liberia, won by blood, sweat and tears

Where're foes assail, we gather to quench
Time after time, we rise above the frail
All hail the land where freedom truly reigns,
My Liberia, my piece of the peace

Reviews

I am delighted to highly commend John Yormie for his book, "Liberia In The Colorful World Of Diplomacy"; a reminder that nothing men do, make or destroy, can lie outside the scope of historical investigation. It is incumbent upon all Liberians to know the pivotal role Liberia played in the comity of nations- that is knowing the past and present role endured to keep our nation in cadence.

Ambassador George W. Wallace, Jr.
Advisor on Foreign Affairs to the President of Liberia

In the book, *Liberia In The Colorful World Of Diplomacy* the author reminds us about Liberia's international relations with the world by making a strong assertion on its historical legacy.
This book is a key introductory literature full of diplomatic perspectives of a tiny nation that has contributed immensely to the world. A highly recommended book.

Dr. Edwin B. R. Gbargaye
Assistant Professor,
Graduate School, University of Liberia

This work provides a valuable and essential lens through which students, diplomats, and Liberian studies enthusiasts will appreciate how the Liberian ship of state sailed faithfully through boisterous oceans of world politics; one characterized by gun boat diplomacy, colonialism and imperialism to assume a place of honor in the colorful world of diplomacy. As a co-founder of the League of Nations, the United Nations, the Organization of African Unity (OAU- now AU), the Mano River Union, (MRU), The African Development Bank (AfDB) and the Economic Community of West African States (ECOWAS) and several more bodies, Liberia remained dsinguished.

Emmanuel Z. Bowier
Former Minister,
Information, Culture and Tourism

Liberia in the Colorful World of Diplomacy

Chapter 1

Dying Legacies Invoked:
Mapping the Significant Roles of Liberia in the International Sphere.

Abstract

A phenomenal progress of mankind, still widely embraced, is the existence of nation states. Tracing from the West Philia Treaty to present, states have been marked by features, which transcend geographic locations and include superficial tenants like rogue states, weak states, developed states among others.

In the comity of nations, each state carves out something that makes it relevant. Liberia, the author argues, has carved out for itself a large portion relative to its size and definitely considering the struggle the nation faced as Africa's lone Republic. Sadly, though, these gains are underplayed, ignored and simply forgotten in some quarters today. Several factors account for that, but for the sake of brevity, we would consider these:

a. **_Shifting of Power_** over time, especially after President Tubman's death, power shifted. President Tubman had structured national diplomacy in a personal way. With him gone and no one groomed, a void was created. There was no concerted effort by the new leader to aggressively galvanize the gains made.

b. **Dwindling Scholarship-** President Tubman for all his flare was no scholar. He did not write down his philosophies as other key players did. This is perhaps his greatest mistake- unlike Ghana's Nkrumah, or his (Tubman's) protégé, President Sekou Toure of Guinea. Generally, scholarship into Liberia's global role became less forthcoming.

c. ***Bureaucratic Reform-*** The new president focused on building a merit-based civil service and undid much of the systemic patronage of his predecessor. This inward look affected scholars and their focus of interest. While President Tolbert fought with an entrenched bureaucracy, globally, the Cold War was peaking. Africa, with its newly independent nations, became the new battlefield. The USA and the USSR tried for as many nations to beef up their respective power bases.

d. ***Civil Unrest and political manipulations.*** By the time President Tolbert had sorted out his internal bureaucratic problem, a new one arose. The years of marginalization by the Settler hegemony and their cohorts, many powerful tribal chiefs, came to a souring point. Political activism, mostly by young scholars hungry for power, hit unprecedented levels. The "Progressives" manipulated the old wounds and instigated major upset for the new president. The largely undereducated population was gullible enough to ensure the agitation worked. President Tolbert barely survived the crisis in time to host the OAU's 1979 Summit held in Liberia. President Tolbert took a hard-handed approach initially and pushed his Liberianization policies, partly underestimating the national class dissent. He believed empowering locals would be worth it. When he slacked off and invited the 'progressives' for talks, they took that to be a sign of weakness and went in for the kill. This tension eventually spilled over to the 1980 coup that toppled the Settler hegemony.

These and several other factors have overshadowed the pivotal role the tiny nation played on the international, continental and regional scenes.

However, the author argues that much has been written about features of the ruining economy, civil war, child mortality, teenage pregnancy and other dreadful situations than the integral roles that Liberia has played in fostering international cooperation and providing for actions aimed at maintaining peace and security, which are core to human existence.

Therefore, this chapter brings together elemental contributions from Liberia towards the formation of international and regional originations, and support to worthy causes of adverting sufferings and degradation against the human race.

An essential part of the chapter identifies ways the African Union (AU) have shaped the dynamics of governance in Africa. We argue that Liberia played a significant and critical role in this achievement.

Background

The name Liberia stems from a Latin word Liber, which means "land of the freed". (Bayor, Ronald, 2011). The country stretches over a land area of 43,000 square (111,369 square kilometers) miles, 23 percent of which is water, with 350 miles of coastline. By the 2015 estimate, Liberia is home to 4,503,000 persons[1].

According to the 2008 National Census, the Kpelle tribe accounts for the most populous tribe at 20.3 percent, followed by Bassa, 13.4; Grebo, 10.0; Gio, 8.0; Mano, 7.9; Kru, 6.0; Lorma, 5.1; Kissi, 4.8; Gola, 4.4; and others, 20.1.

Liberia is located on the west coast of Africa and shares borders with Guinea to the north; Sierra Leone to the West; Ivory Coast to the east; and the Atlantic Ocean to the south. Much of the climate is dry or wet rainy seasons.

Introduction

With more than a century and half of existence as a sovereign nation state, Liberia's journey has covered millions of miles. Liberia has a soft spot among the earliest driving forces in the formation of key international organizations and significant international instruments. Liberia was the only African state at the function forming the League of Nations in Paris in 1920.

---

[1] "Liberia". The World Fact book. Central Intelligence Agency

At the San Francisco conference, Liberia was also a founding member of the UN (Liberia's representatives who signed the charter: C.L. Simpson Sr. – Chairman, Gabriel L. Dennis, Lemuel Gibson, Richard A. Henries and Moses Grant).

Regionally, Liberia is a founding member of the Mano River Union (MRU) and the Economic Community of West Africa States (ECOWAS); while continentally, it played key roles in the Organization of African Unity (OAU) now, the African Union (AU).

On the peacekeeping front, Liberia, in 1961, provided troops to the United Nations' Congo Operation – a UN peacekeeping force established under UN Security Council Resolution 143 of July 14, 1960 to respond to the Congo crisis. For that mission, Liberia sent forces on two occasions, and everyone returned home safely in evidence to fostering peace and cooperation, which is central to the UN.

Liberia, through contributions to international organizations, positioned itself to gain from the future. By its early support, Liberia displayed functional utilities in the international sphere and gained more than just favorable commendation but also a status as a key player at many of these organizations. For example,

Liberia produced the only female president of the United Nations General Assembly from Africa, Angie E. Brooks Randall- one of only two females globally.

Mrs. Brook Randall served in other key positions, including Vice Chairperson of the Committee on Information for non-self governing Territories (colonies of European powers, which was instituted to address concerns of Africa on the agenda of the General Assembly.

She served also as the chairperson of the Fourth Committee of the General Assembly as well as the Chairperson of the Special Committee on the issue of Burundi-Urundi which was a Belgium Trust Territory later divided into Burundi and Rwanda in 1962. She can be hailed for fostering the admission of many African Nations States to the UN in the early 1960s during the rise of sovereign African States.

Today, the significance of international organizations has been identified by scholars and international actors including, Breme Allemagne, who points out that international

Organizations and International Non-Governmental Organizations (INGOs) have played a leading role in the making of global development policies during the last fifty years and are powerful engines of globalization as well as global transmitters of ideas and knowledge.

This has become more convincing as the roles of these organizations become increasingly more pronounced and recognized by governmental actors of the most powerful countries.

Similarly, Esther Brimmer, a U.S. Assistant Secretary of State for International Organizations at the State Department, noted, "ultimately it is about shared responses to shared challenge working with international organizations is fundamentally essential to modern diplomacy. International organizations are places where nations can find common solutions to complex problems."

Formation of Organization of African Unity-OAU- and Contextual Relevance

Historically, Liberia has, for a long time, played meaningful roles in organizing civilized patterns of human existence, especially regional or global institutions and organizations. While knowing about the League of Nations and the United Nations is key, a historical context of Africa is viewed from the formation of the OAU, transitioned to the AU, as well as political support to Nigeria and South Africa.

Both states are competitively Africa's biggest economies. (GDP in South Africa over US$300 billion in 2017, according to Trading Economics global macro models and analysts expectations, while the Gross Domestic Product (GDP) in Nigeria was worth US$481.07 billion in 2015, according to the same source).

Whether Africa is truly independent is a worthy question to save for later while necessity for independence among African countries is considered valid.

Independence gave rise to new nation states in Africa and eventually led to a free Africa devoid of direct colonial rule. This being a legacy to celebrate is incomplete without Liberia. Liberia must be a champion to remember in all of Africa's history, especially pertaining to the liberation struggle.

No serious mention of the formation of the Organization of African Unity (OAU) can be entertained without specific mention to three giant figures on the continent at the time of its creation- the TNT [Tubman, Nkrumah and Toure]. TNT may be more popular as a medical acronym for an antibiotic, but here it refers to a conference that set the pace of the OAU in the historic county capital of Nimba, Sanniquellie, in 1959 depicting Tubman, Nkrumah and Toure. (Horton, R. 2004).

At the behest of Africa's only republic, the leaders of Ghana and Guinea attended the conference.

This signaled to the west not only a uniquely defiant Africa, but also one skilled enough in international diplomacy to call the rest of the world out for actions and inactions to their nations and peoples. The loudness of this message was frightening to colonial masters. They saw in those talks, a child grown enough to want to try life on its own two feet.

During these discussions, two cardinal, inseparable developmental tenets were considered. Economics– leading to the African

Development Bank and politics-leading to the OAU. The genesis of unity and freedom in Africa stemmed from the Sanniquellie meeting, where all the leaders agreed to foster a fully independent and united Africa. (ibid).

Poised to the fulfillment of the agenda, another meeting in 1961 was also convened by Tubman in welcoming newly independent states into the comity of nations. That eventually led to the drafting of the charters of the AfDB and the OAU, signed and coming into force in 1963. Dismally, these meetings have all but faded from the formative chapters of these institutions.

Current Trends

Since then, the African Development Bank has played pivotal roles in addressing phenomenon economic issues in Liberia and Africa at large. Now the bank lends to fragile states and offers low interest loans to countries. It has a special fund for the fight against some of the world's killer diseases. The long envisioned dreams of the great men of Liberia, with continental shared-inclusiveness, for a united and economically prosperous Africa is well a reality to celebrate. Areas of priority for the AfDB include social development by developing infrastructure like power supply, water, sanitation, transport, and communication. From research at the end of 2015, the Bank had made US$112 billion off loans and grants since 1967, through some 4,370 operations. In 2015, it disbursed US$ 8.8 billion in 240 operations.

The AU, as an offspring of Liberia's brainchild, has some objectives to achieve. These include greater unity and solidarity between the African countries and Africans; to defend the sovereignty, territorial integrity and independence of its Member States; to accelerate the political and socioeconomic integration of the continent; to promote and defend African common positions on issues of interest; its peoples, which are now influencing governance in Africa.

Today, the AU has supported several peacekeeping missions and created regimes in support of a wider framework of democracy. Its functionaries resisted violent governments in Mali and Burkina Faso, further ensuring the dream Liberia had over half a century ago. The African-led International Support Mission in Mali (AFISMA), to which Liberia contributes troops, is also a fulfillment of maintaining the territorial integrity of Member States of AU, like the AU/UN Hybrid in Sudan.

Major Assumptions

Two of Africa's biggest economies owe a wealth of gratitude to Liberia. For example, Nigeria was supported by Liberia in gaining political sovereignty; while the fight to bring relief to marginalized South Africans, in the struggle against the Apartheid system, was hugely influenced by Liberia, even to the extent of affording refuge and finances to one of the world's most affluent and cross cutting societal figures, Nelson R. Mandela. Same was afforded to huge Masekela and Mariam Makeba and tons of other freedom fighters in the South African struggle. (An Interview with Amb. George W. Wallace, September 2018) (also AVAILABLE AT https://www.sahistory.org.za/article/1960s-diaries-nelson-mandela-his-trip-through-africa. 1960s Diaries of Nelson Mandela on his trip throughout Africa).

Domestic policy implementation and infrastructure still lag in Liberia as compared to most parts of Africa thereby creating a diminished feature of Liberia's international image.

The roles of professional Liberians at sub-regional, regional and International Governmental Organizations like MRU, ECOWAS and AU, have over the recent years taken a downward turn.

Conclusion

The chapter discussed some of the important roles Liberia has played in international diplomacy with emphasis on international and regional organizations [UN, OAU/AU, MRU etc.].

In spite of the undeniable role that Liberia played in the independence processes of South Africa and Nigeria, the author is aware that it will be erroneous to mention that the levels of growth and development both have obtained are based directly on Liberia.

The author argues mostly to the fact that the stages, which led to both countries' fundamental political stability, have important traces to the roles Liberia played in setting their political systems.

Endnotes

Encyclopedia of World Geography, 2000). New York: Barnes & Noble Books. p. 161. ISBN 1-56619-291-9.)
Bayor, Ronald, 2011). Multicultural America: An Encyclopedia of the Newest Americans, Volume 2.)

"Liberia". The World Fact book. Central Intelligence Agency

1. **Discuss some methods of diplomacy employed by Liberia in the early African liberation movement.**

2. **What do you think accounts for the 'erasure' of the Liberian narrative in the formation of these international bodies?**

3. **How the rise in technology and globalization is influencing Liberia's Diplomacy as compared to its traditional State to State Diplomacy?**

4. **By whom and why Sanniquellie was selected for the meeting?**

Chapter 2

Cultural Diplomacy and MRU

Relationships are fundamental social phenomena of humanity- be they based on blood ties, sharing common spaces, or other forms of social fraternities. The disciplines of sociology and international relations play major roles in understanding that which binds society. They focus on more than just the fundamentals; they delve into the crux of socially constructed tenants and other inherent societal factors, which shift group dynamics.

For example, the French Sociologist Emile Durkheim coined the term *mechanical solidarity* to explain how social bonds, based on common sentiments and shared moral values emphasizing tradition, generate a cohesive pattern. This is something essentially associated with rural live. (Macionis, J.; 2004). Hence, lending credence to claims that significant aspects of international relations are historically and socially constructed, rather than inevitable consequences of human nature or other essential characteristics of the world politics (Jackson, P.T. &Nixon, H.).

Constructivists like Alexander Wendt argue the significance of norms, values and their influence on structures. He espouses that "the structure of human association are determined primarily by shared ideals rather than material forces and identities and interest of purposive actors are constructed on these shared ideas rather than given nature" (Wendt, A.; 1999).

Therefore, the chapter explores how shared values bind political entities of similar nature. It postulates the context based on the sub-regional integration of the Mano River Union (MRU) with lessons learned from the European Union (EU) as a regional organization.

It firstly identifies cultural diplomacy as a crucial factor that binds nations considering the intricate significance of national security and establishes how this can be applicable in the MRU region, also providing the contextual relevance and prospects of the same.

Introduction

Cultural diplomacy is a type of public diplomacy and soft power that includes exchange of ideas, information, art and other aspects of culture among nations and peoples in order to foster mutual understanding (Waller J.M, 2009 p.74). The work to achieve the state's political and economic interests can be built through cultural diplomacy as it has been argued by Mary N. Maack in her piece "Books and Libraries as Instruments for Cultural Diplomacy in francophone Africa During the Cold War" (Maack, M. N., 2001).

Waller's argument that cultural diplomacy can also be linked to national security comes from his assertion that the perception of power obviously has important implications for a nation's ability to ensure its security (Waller, J.M; 2009 p. 93).

The Mano River Union (MRU) is an international association with a sub-regional identity established in 1973 between Liberia and Sierra Leone with the goal of fostering economic cooperation. Guinea joined in 1980 and later, in 2008, Cote D'Ivoire joined the Union.

Similarly, the European Union was founded with the aim of ending wars, fought across Europe. Regional cooperation among neighbors was fundamental to its creation. Since its formation early 1950s, by the European Coal and Steel Community [aimed at centrally tailoring unity for European countries] the EU has focused on political stability and economic prosperity.

Originally, the union comprised the Netherlands, Luxembourg, France, Belgium, Germany, and Italy. Currently EU members amount to about 28 states.

Thus, it can be agreed that the fostering of peace amongst states of Europe, which were constantly at war with each other, was essential to the formation of the European Union (EU).

Analysis

This section views the structural relativities of the MRU with the EU and identifies areas of prospects of the MRU.

In accounting for man's existence, the account of wars covers significant amount of human history. The triggers have differed across many societies. Claude Waltz describes war as the extension of politics by other means; while cultural anthropologist Margret Mead associated war with "inborn tendency"- asserting that war is an innate characteristic that is passed on from one generation to another.

While these postulations may be argued, the history of wars in countries of the MRU stands as factual accounts. Each country has experienced some form of mass violence or civil conflict. At some point in time, the situation began because of the psychological perception, "mirror image". Each saw the other as an existential threat to the other.

During the 1900s the early 2000s, the entire sub region was in a state of disarray. The perennial *threat* seemed real to many due to allegedly frequent cross borders attacks. The view of peaceful co –existence, which amongst member countries is a foreign policy tool, was at the lowest while animosity and acrimonious sentiments became so common. This was quite challenging and disallowed free movement and cross border trade.

The question is after these years of turmoil, are there prospects of greater collaboration and integration or what are the fundamental problems, which have existed?

Historical efficacies, which provide broader insights to answering these questions, will take various dimensions including a classical example of the organization of the European Union.

Despite the awful past of continuous wars across Europe, the establishment of the European Union has manifested the outcome of peace, stability and economic prosperity. This has precipitated many things including more than 60 years of peace and stability, helped raise population's living standards, launched a single currency (the euro) and making progress on building a single Europe-wide market for goods, services, people and capital.

After many years of regional instability in Europe, the establishment of norms and values that led to a regional organization, thereafter stabilizing Europe, can be articulated as a socially constructed phenomenon against the odds of wars. This can also be applied to the MRU region with some fundamental factors.

Aligned with the above case study, firstly is the argument that there are key factors, which propel growth, subsequently peace and economic prosperity. They include political stability, education, health, economics etc.

Education in the entire region still appears more challenging whereas economic situations of inequalities are alarming.

To address the concern of spiraling economic mechanisms, political stability is crucial and will depend on a number of factors. "People- to -people relationship" is vital, something herein describes as "foot path diplomacy": the interaction of close relatives along borderlines despite geographical boundaries.

Education can change the thinking of populations and easily promote policy out looks. This is crucial for the region. When these factors are put in place, trade is bound to boom as inter trade routes are multiplied in the region.

Therefore, how the real deal of pragmatism can surcease? It can by ascending toward the mentioned goals align with cultural diplomacy in ways that support exchanges of students, projection of policy and issues through arts and cultural displays. Another way is by teaching local languages of member states in the region to all member states to reduce language barriers.

Since the 2004 reactivation summit, the Union has experienced renewed assurances of collaboration at various levels. Prospects are huge, as the region's population, mostly comprises of youths, which would turn out to be more productive when afforded the requisite education at various levels- including Technical Vocational Education and Training (TVET).

Major Assumptions

The hostilities in the member state stalled free trade movement while "mirror image "reduced free movement thus affecting track III- people to people diplomacy. This can be revamped by increased cultural diplomacy. Despite issues of land areas, which have existed amongst member states, the conflicts in the MRU region were more political than ontological and deeply associated with the post -cold war effects that saw violent internal conflicts across Africa. Thus, the prospect for greater collaborations shows with evident track for peaceful co-existence while the cutting-edge of economic viability is highly certain, all things being constant.

Conclusion

The chapter identified what holds society together in the context of bringing nation states together under the framework of integration and regional solidarity. The situation of civil war in the region was discussed describing the nature of the wars. The success of the EU region post regional conflict was mentioned in an attempt to validate the significance of socially constructed structures as well as the relevance to cultural diplomacy.

Thus, Cultural diplomacy is the crux of the paper and stands as a recommended approach to spur people-to-people cohesiveness, which affirms support to peace and upsurge free movements that give rise to economic activities. To maintain the peace and promote innovation and expertise as well as sound policy orientations, focus on education was emphasized with the assertion that many people still face challenges of access to quality education in the region.

1. What possible steps can regional leaders take to improve interregional growth?

2. What lessons can the MRU learn from the European Union? Discuss.

3. Discuss the MRU in terms of future growth prospects in the area of free movement of people, goods and services.

4. Discuss the significance of shared local languages in the MRU area?

Chapter 3

Human Security: Aligning Domestic and Foreign Policies

Introduction

Freedom reigns in movements and speeches but how indicative are the elements of being glorious when considering economic prosperity, social welfare and infrastructural development, which are all essential to sustainable development and human security?

In an attempt to focus on the significance of Human Security, the paper gives a dual view on the need to align domestic and foreign policies, to ensure the achievement of better living for a defined population; Liberians in this case.

Born out of free slaves from the United States of America (USA), formerly referred to as the Pepper Coast because of its greenery, the Republic of Liberia officially joined the comity of nations on July 26, 1847 with three original counties (Montserrado, Grand Bassa and Sinoe) (Guannu, J; 2010).

Now the defined territory of Liberia covers 15 political subdivisions/counties with a population estimated at over 4 million according to recent World Bank report. It is bounded on the west by Sierra Leone, south by the Atlantic Ocean, east by the Ivory Coast and north the Republic of Guinea. The country can be widely remembered for its role in ensuring an independent Africa with particular support to end the civil war in Nigeria (Biafran war) and apartheid in South Africa.

Today, both countries account for two of the biggest economies in Africa by GDP measure with the former at$594.257 billion and the latter 341.216 as of recent estimates. (Available at https://naijaquest.com/largest-economies-in-africa, retrieved May12, 2018). Liberia's foreign policy is firmly rooted in its political ideology of liberalism, democracy and capitalism. This foundation is copied after the pattern adopted by the USA from which the founding fathers of Liberia had come as free men of color.

The guiding principles of Liberia's foreign policy has been:

- *the maintenance of national security*
- *the preservation of the territorial integrity*
- *sovereignty of the country,*

In addition, there is the promotion of peace based on the principle of non-interference in the internal affairs of other states, and unity in the international community based on liberal democracy.

Liberia's survival as a state in the face of difficult challenges posed by colonial powers like Great Britain and France have been the skills and maturity with which its leaders conducted foreign policy and foreign relations. Thus, the mastery of the act of diplomacy has remained the hallmark, and one of the most credible achievements of Liberia in the comity of nations. (Available at www.emansion.gov.lr retrieved August 15, 2016).

Human Security is a paradigm linked to understanding global vulnerabilities that challenge the notion of only national security with an argument that proper reference for security should be the individual rather than the state. The idea revolves around insuring that "freedom from want" and "freedom from fear" for all persons is the best path to tackle problem of global security. (UNDP Report, 1994).

Analysis

A nation's foreign policy- consists of self-interest strategies chosen by the state to safeguard its national interests and to achieve goals within its international relations milieu (Morgenthau, H. J.; 1967).

Functionally, foreign policy is an extension of domestic policy, which is an embodiment of a country's national interest. Domestic policy is cradled on administrative decisions that are directly related to all issues and activity within a nation's borders. (ibid).

Therefore, Liberia's foreign policy formulation, and implementation must align with the country's vital national interests reflective of the needs of the average citizenry (education, health, electricity, water and roads etc.). Meanwhile, its alignments with powerful countries or development of bilateral relations must be based on bargaining, not mere recipient of good will, which many times amount to unexpressed exploitation which are only realized after a long period of time. The fundamental thrust of Liberia's foreign policy objective before the Tubman era was predominantly the maintenance of national independence.

Since the Tubman administration to date, the foreign policy objective of the country, in addition to the maintenance of sovereignty, has been the devotion to economic, social and political development. It was further advanced to development diplomacy under Madam Sirleaf.

Considering the changing natures and shifting dynamics, seeking for trade partnerships, other than just aid, must be a path to tread. It is based on the ideological construct that aid subjects the recipient and reduces the choices of the aid dependent.

These are viewed from the constraints of aid conditionality and limitation of the receiving state to tailor project based on needs but the adherence patterns from the donors. The proponent in reverse is when a country identifies its potential to attract investment and secure trade partners. These will depend on preconditions of principal negotiators and actors of the foreign policy agenda to mirror the country's image of:

- *rule of law*
- *the protection of intellectual properties*
- *ease of doing business and*
- *plausible determinants of growth engines (roads, electricity, water, etc).*

The role of government relations with the media is very important to spur public diplomacy in this regard. For instance, when a nation's foreign policy is built on the above

Fulbright Scholarships
Exchange of professors
Joint research projects
Existing security sector

Support will increase with the developed world. Even Chinese multinational firms will invest more in agriculture, railways, solar energy and reduction in barriers to trade in the Mano River Union (MRU) region will suffice just to mention a few. These will stimulate the necessary conditions that promote human security with the drive of elevating the social welfare of the average citizens. Considering the relationship between the domestic and foreign policies, the national interest can be parallel to the vital interest expressed in the formulation and conduct of foreign policy.

Thus, it is important to provide a safe guide here that national security is not being ignored here but rather looked at from a different way; which is by focusing on human security as a foundation for national security.

One key aspect of human security is health. Of the many challenges faced by Liberia, the health sector is among the most appalling. This strand is critical and invariable to the survival of a functioning society. But it can be argued that, not much has been engendered in advancing health issues in Liberia's foreign policy. It has been asserted that for human security to challenge global inequalities there has to be cooperation between a country's foreign policy and its approach to global health. (Spiegel, J.M. and Huish, R.; 2009).

Major Assumptions

The concept of developing variables of human security are still centered on aid dependency and signifies a void of a national will to stimulate negotiations or trade agreements that accelerate growth. This leads to a development plan, which has positive marriage to increase government revenues and individual living conditions that reflect human security.

Under the Reducing Emission Deforestation and Degradation of Forest (REDD plus) program for developing countries, having stock of carbon is an attractive value. Liberia contains in forest areas approximately 585 million metric tons of carbon in living biomass (available at https://rainforests.mongabay.com/deforestatio n/2000/Liberia.htm).

Having such abundant stock of carbon positions the country high on the discussion table. But it can be argued that the bargaining skills and assess to require knowledge has not yielded the surmountable dividends in negotiating internationally. The country is yet to reap significant programs that will transcend to the average poor; thus addressing concerns of human security, at least, through that program.

Conclusion and Recommendations

This chapter streamlined the complementary of foreign and domestic polices, centrally asserting that, elements of the former must be aligned with the latter whereby the national interest must be the core of its formulation and implementation.

It identifies the validity of national security but asserts that when much attention is paid only to national security, in terms of defense of borders and nationhood, the void of human security deepens and thereby has adverse effects causing fragility to the same national security being protected.

Thus, with the continued collaborations, especially in the Mano River Union region, and Economic Community of West African States (ECOWAS), evident to the existing ECOWAS passport, West African power pool project and increased joint commissions which focus exchange of knowledge, agriculture development etc., the threat of external aggression can be considered unlikely despite possibilities of insurgence and terrorist activities.

Therefore, while achieving these, programs which cover safety nets for the poor must be looked at in addition to the provision of low income housing, improving health facilities etc. with consistency in domestic and foreign policy agendas.

1. Discuss how national policy ties in with foreign policy.

2. How does human security affect national security? Discuss

3 Describe the standards of public diplomatic training and how they are aiding Foreign Service Officers (FSOs) to attract opportunities that support human security

4 Discuss the process of domesticating international instruments/regimes Liberia signs on to.

5 Discuss how political will of the President of Liberia affects formulation and implementation of foreign policy

Chapter 4

Rethinking Liberia's Polices and Politics: Liking the Past with Present

Abstract

How can we view politics and policies? How they interplay to affect the society? Especially thinking of man's innate desire to control or seek compliance from others. (Randy, R. and Buss David M; 2010).

It is even intensified when fueled by manipulations of poor and uneducated populations, which apparently the political scene Liberia is colored by. (Poverty rate 54% of Liberians live below the poverty line (available at http.www.allafrica.com 2016).

Policies may be defined as courses, principles or actions adopted or proposed by a government, party, business or individual (Oxford Advanced Learners Dictionary New 7th edition).

S. Torjman states, "we literally eat, drink and breath polices which are public in nature thereby affecting the quality of life we live" (Torjman S., 2005). The argument here is that policies are critical to whatever we do.

Meanwhile, Clausewitz the classical German political theorist addresses the issue from a somewhat different angle. He suggests war as continuation of politics/policy. It is another means, which may be more contentious, nonetheless, it is an activity associated with governance. Unfavorable, this may be, especially considering the debate on conflict resolution, yet it is a means to achieve power.

Thus, the author argues that regardless the position one takes on the matter, the effectiveness of policies depend largely on the factors, which influence the political system. This can be seen in the case of Liberia. From as early as pre independence, the domestic politics of the young nation, as well as major public policies, have been dented by mere politics.

Liberia gained its independence on July 26, 1847 having amongst several reasons the need for self-governance as main cause. Although over time, the American Colonization Society (ACS), which was its principal institution steering the administrative affairs, became bankrupt and forced the Common Wealth to early independence.

Analysis:

The Conundrum of Aged Problems

Dating back to the 19th century, Liberia emerged out of three counties (Montserrado, Grand Bassa and Sinoe) and later annexed Cape Mount and Maryland but had a continuous formation of new counties between the 60s-80s. Gradually, other counties were formed- with River Gee and Gbarpolu being the most recent (Available here http://www.mia.gov.lr/ retrieved March 20, 2017), thus concluding its formation.

Population-wise, from about 3,000 persons, during the formative stages, to a now estimated 4 million[2], should be evidence of how Liberia has evolved, from a tiny colony of little significance, to a major player on the global scene as covered in the first chapter.

---

[2]Liberia Population (2019) World meters (www.worldometers.info) estimates Liberia's population over 4.5 million, still having rubber and iron ore as major commodities.

Policy wise

The argument is that, Liberia is not far advanced, than in its formative years, in terms of policy. It is riddled with systemic issues of, decentralization, Information Communication Technology (ICT), basic technology and road connectivity. It seems trapped in a loop of growth without development- a state of massive aid but limited development as in the 60s.

Aid, Concession and Unequal Economy

Trending is the issue of Concessions. Now, with limited corporate social responsibilities, the impact of such deals resembles the 1926 Firestone agreement. A factor of note is that Liberia, between 2005 and 2015, averaged more than a Billion dollars in aid; with 2011 alone accounting for 765 million from OECD alone, but she still faces major challenges with road networks. There are only 6.2km of paved primary roads according recent World Bank data, coupled with access to inadequate health care and limited learning opportunities to match the demand for a highly literate population.

Between 1822 and 1839, Liberia (as a colony) experienced very slow economic development mainly because there were no highways from which produce from the hinterland to the coastal areas could be transported. This was then the epic zones of international trade, (Guannu, J.S.; 2010).

Today most parts of Liberia remain without paved roads, which undermine economic development, especially during the rainy season. Like the coastal areas in the past. It can be argued that most of the economic activities are still concentrated in Monrovia and with stark difficulties associated with getting produce to Monrovia (the Nation's Capital) from the hinterlands. This aged problem still lingers.

In all this, very few Liberians had money to start their own businesses while a significant number preferred government work to business (ibid). Although in the early 1920s, trade and commerce experienced an upsurge in Liberian ownership, the introduction of more sophisticated hardware by Germans and Dutch traders, forced low skilled Liberia artisans and salesmen out of business as mentioned in "A brief History of Montserrado County" by Henries D.B, Moore B.T et al.

Understandably, foreign traders had more capital to invest than their local counterparts, despite the skills factor did. Evidently, the story has not changed as exemplified by the growth of government. Government remains the single biggest employer [Labor Ministry].

The Rice Factor

For most part of Liberia's history, rice has been its staple food. But to imagine that 90% of products (including rice) consumed in Liberia are imported, raises more questions and call for serious concerns.

However, it may be more of a surprise to many that Liberia produced one of best varieties of rice until what the author describes as *unmatched western agricultural intervention* altered the mode of production.

In Noam Chomsky's book, "Year -501 The Conquest Continues", he explains Anthropologist Gordon Thomasson discovery of how hundreds of varieties of rice matched precisely to the micro environments in particular ecosystems developed by the Kpelle. This trend was discontinued due to US agronomists advised capital-intensive Green revolution techniques. These methods used petrochemical inputs, which apart from being far too costly for a poor country brought lower yields and loss of traditional knowledge.

It further affected the wide variety of seeds that have been bred, selected, diversified and maintained over centuries. He described this as Irrational Disdain for Native Intellectual Achievement (Chomsky; N., 1993).

He further estimated that as the result, agriculture productivity would be cut by 50 present if the rich genetic pool of rice varieties is lost and replaced by foreign inputs something, which corroborates with high imports of rice over locally produced rice in Liberia presently.

To follow how policies have been formulated to change the story, and were subsequently overturned by politics, the infamous 1979 rice riot can be revisited.

Understandably, President Tolbert had realized that until local farmers are empowered to produce rice, Liberia will continue to feed on foreign inputs. Liberia needed to be food sufficient; there was no doubt about that. So, he created schemes to empower local farmers. Building on the famous "Rally Time National Policy", he increased tariffs on foreign inputs, which then caused a rise in the price of rice from 22 USD to 26 USD for 50 Kg bag of rice, something that would obviously have a transitional growth period before the actualization of desired outcomes.

Despite the intent, it was negatively politicized by politicians and ultimately led to a massive uprising on April 14, 1979. An otherwise decent policy went to waste merely because it was politicized.

Major Assumptions

The situation to test the empowerment policy of local farmers was not given adequate time for maturity. Instead, it was rather manipulated to create domestic tension. As tariffs are placed on essentials goods, shortages may occur; when such happens, demands ceiling and prices follow same pattern.

One may argue that putting tariffs at that moment was not necessary but the price was affordable. In addition, considering the intent of the policy, to empower local farmers, it should have, at least, been allowed to play out.

Amongst the many problems is the issue of unemployment-, especially when youth focused. This is something, which is a global concern. Skills development then becomes a major strand to follow, in aspiration to first, set the preparedness premise that illustratively leads to world of work.

This supposedly means that government should prioritize, within youth empowerment programs, skills development and higher education encompassing Technical Vocational Education and Training and Information Communication Technology.

These are likely to empower young people for a quick transition. These mere *roadside brushing*, are just physical community short term impact-projects, lacking long-term sustainable development incentives. This will enhance production and entrepreneurship to drive competition of Liberians with foreign businesses.

Conclusion

The chapter outlined a few examples of a historical trend of protracted problems- with the argument that negative politics have undermined significant polices. It identified some causes [in select areas] for which Liberian businesses have suffered limited capacities to compete considering skills and adequate capital acquisition to invest.

It unpacked a broad focus on failure to address sectors of the society, which drive growth and development including education, convenient road connectivity and sustainable agricultural practices.

1. **What could have been done differently with the protectionist policy President Tolbert employed in the rice industry? Discuss.**

2. **Youth employment, the way forward. Discuss.**

3. **How can the aged old problem of importing significantly large amounts of basic goods many foods products be addressed?**

4. **Have Liberians nationals found their right place in entrepreneurship in the economy of Liberia? If yes explain how and if no explain why**

Chapter 5

Reforms in Public Bureaucratic Structures in Liberia Since 2005

The Liberian governance system has experienced significant reforms over the decade from 2005 to 2015. The establishment and revitalization of bodies like the General Auditing Commission (GAC), the Liberia Anti-Corruption Commission (LACC), as well as the formation of the Executive Protective Service (EPS) evidences this. There have also been administrative restructuring of the Liberia National Police (LNP) [among others by legislative enactments.]

These reforms have spread across the three branches of government. For instance, in the Judiciary, the introduction of the National Public Defense program through the Public Defenders'

Office (PDO), under the direct coordination of a Coordinator for Public Defense is a clear case. This was necessitated in attribution to observance and domestication of several international instruments including the right to competent, independent and impartial tribunal in articulated in the Universal Declaration of Human Rights (UDGR, Art.10) and the International Covenant on Civil and Political Rights(ICCPR Art 14). (Available at http://judiciary.gov.lr/public-defence/)

Also at the Legislature the , the Legislative Modernization Plan 2009-2013 also produced the Legislative Budget Office(LBO) fully funded and staffed to provide technical support to the legislature on the formulation of the National budget. (Available at https://www.liberianlawmakerswatch.org/.../modernization plan 2009.pdf

Whether as the offspring of the Comprehensive Peace Agreement (CPA) recommendation in 2003, aid conditionality or demands for national policy outlook, this chapter explores how two major entities have shown the significance of systems reform. Under the continuum of reform, the Liberia Revenue Authority (LRA) and the Public Procurement and Concession Commission (PPCC) are cases of structural reforms worth noting. Chapter five also discusses how entities, when properly structured, can resuscitate income and boost cost effectiveness on public goods and services.

The LRA was established by an Act of Legislature in 2013 and began operations on July 1, 2014. (LRA Corporate Strategic Plan Fiscal Years 2016/17-2020/21).

It replaced the department of Revenue of the then Ministry of Finance (Including the Bureau of Internal Revenue and the Bureau of Customs and Excise) as defined in Chapter 21 of the Executive Law of 1972.

Its primary purpose is to assess and collect national revenue as specified in the Revenue Code of Liberia or related law. It is responsible for administering accounting, auditing and enforcing revenue collection laws and regulations, and educating taxpayers to facilitate tax and customs compliance. (LRA Act available at (www.lra.gov.lr)

On the other hand, The PPCC Act of 2005, amended in 2010, established the PPCC to regulate all forms of public procurement and concessions. It provides for institutional structures for public procurement and concessions, and stipulates methods and procedures for public procurement and concessions and for purposes related thereto. (PPCC Act available at www.ppcc.gov.lr).

Analysis

At an estimated population of 4.2 million, Liberia in August of 2014 experienced nominal growth rate averaged at 5.5 percent for four years running. It also averaged 74.6% vulnerable employment and registered limitations in options for more meaningful employment and financing of investment opportunities.

Publicly supplied electricity then reached less than 5% of the population, at a cost of around USD 54 cents per kWh, something which renders manufacturing absurdly expensive as compared to neighbors (Guinea: 16.4 USD cents/KWh, Ivory Coast : 13.9USD, Sierra Leone : 25 cents per kWh; available at World Bank- Doing Business).

Privately supplied power, often more costly, estimated at USD 70 cent per KWh according to word Bank Report 2014. Only 6% percent of the total road network then paved, and much of the country's interior is cut off from the capital during the rainy season.

However, Plans are underway to construct new roads, including Gbarnga- Mendikorma, Ganta –Tappita, Zwedru-Fish Town and several localities in Liberia.

Mostly, these data do not show a favorable economy nor a society on a buildup of industrialization, which are the citizens' quest.

So realizing how significant projects are, as well as having the funds and ability to provide the needed services, to ensure full delivery, adequate income generation and smart spending appear inevitable. Thus, the LRA and the PPCC epitomize positive trends.

Just as someone working in a developed country expects tax payment as a way of life, others in developing nations should be able to do same.

Beyond the individual, public sector imperatives do exist. Government must generate and spend money for the public, therefore getting the money and spending it, lie in effecting public sector revenue collection, spending and functioning.

The LRA contributes 70% to the revenue pot and its functions to assessing and collecting national revenue have greatly helped.

In justification of its establishment, the LRA raised a landmark income of about 19.9 million- by raising 437.2 million, 4.6 percent above its target for domestic tax collection [initially passed at 417.2 million] - in its first year of operation.

Although comparing public and private sectors may somewhat appear redundant, the parallels usually scout the notch of comparison.

In the private sector, procurement is viewed as a strategic function to improve the organization's profitability and as helping to stream line processes; reduce raw materials prices, and cost and identifying better sources of supply in essence of helping to reduce the bottom line.

However, in the Public sector, bottom line is less well defined where as there are no shareholders' dividend to be paid out or publicly declared profit or loss.

But teaching and research have been recommended to maximize output within available funds. In this manner, a relation can be established by making taxpayers like shareholders. This demands the accountability as well as value for money.

At the higher level, key elements needed are for expenditure; the need for openness, transparency and non- discrimination, backed by required legislation. As discussed By Christopher H. Bovis in his book, "The EU and Public Procurement Law" similar tenants are prescribed in the PPCC Act part V under Method of Procurement. There is a need to make public procurement transparent. It shall be undertaken by means of advertised, open bid proceedings, to which equal access shall be provided to all eligible, qualified persons/entities without discrimination, subject only to the exceptions.

Major Assumptions

Ensuring the prowess of procurement officers are well to date with methods, ICT applications will accelerate efficiency at the PPCC.

Employing high tax when new policies like the Small Business Administration Act (http://www.moci.gov.lr)/ are established to encourage domestic entrepreneurs may look good for fast recovery in a period of financial constraints but also largely undermines growth for new businesses. For example the spirit of the Small Business Administration Act to promote Micro Small and Medium enterprises(MSMEs) to reduce poverty by increasing economic growth with a rationale to strengthen small businesses in Liberia, create more private sector employment opportunities, address poverty challenges and develop a robust middle class are undermined by levying high taxes. It further encourages smuggling in a country like Liberia, which to larger extent, faces porous borders problems.

It becomes more problematic by adding that the average of 32% of GDP comes from domestic tax and grants, leaving 19.4% tax ratio when grants and borrowing are excluded – Thereby making a tight fiscal space.

Therefore, high taxation is at an odd with attraction for increasing the fiscal space, which is necessary for revenue generation.

Conclusion and Recommendation

The chapter identified reform measures, which have been taken to boost effective governance from the period of 2005 to 2015. Considering the tight economic variables, generating mass income and spending public funds to acquire the value for money are key; thereby showing up for the strengthening of LRA and PPCC, which have showed cased significance.

Among many measures, to sophisticate ICT systems can be recommended at both entities. Regular up date of the vendor registry on the PPCC website as well as advertisement of contracts and awards and routine stages and accompanying steps (Identification of goods required, preparation of plans for acquisition of goods, invitation of bids, receiving of bids, evaluation of bids). Seeking of approval for contract awards up to performance monitoring must be considered appropriately.

1. **Public sector reform is important for growth. Considering the Liberian case, how significant is the role of the Liberia Revenue Authority (LRA) to a low-based tax system?**

2. **What steps can the LRA take to increase the tax base and collect revenue without upsetting the fragile balance?**

3. **Procurement remains a challenge for any administration (private and government sectors); what specific challenges do the PPCC face? How can they navigate around them?**

Chapter 6

Existing with Limited Efficacies: Corporate Social Responsibility (CSR) and the Liberian Scenario

Abstract

Thinking of state existence from a one-dimensional perspective is not only antiquated but in total distance from the current understanding of statehood. Ever since the rise of international organizations, state- to -state diplomacy has experienced significant changes. It is impossible to miss the upsurge of new players and their insurmountable increase of influence, for example of Multi-national corporations- one can clearly see how the world around us has evolved.

This has also depicted new trends of problems solving globally with conferral of some key roles on corporate entities. Paul Colliers argues the significance of CSR. He notes that efforts from multilateral entities, traditional governments are yet to solve the problems of global poverty, though some gains were made, thus allowing for intervention of businesses in the area of development (Collier, 2007).

This will depend on guided polices and effective implementation on CSR under the watch of National Governments as it may be argued.

Thus, this chapter explores how CSR has evolved as an important concept of the society and argues the significance of corporate entities through CSR. Worthy of note is the fact that the discussion of the concept is limited to Liberia with particular focus on the extractive industry (Mineral Development Agreements).

Introduction

The average Liberian may not be fond of CRS but it plays a major role in development. It is more than just a political phenomenon but a true driver of the economy, which spurs education, social welfare, and of course, employment opportunities by integrating corporate entities and national governments for immediate benefits of host communities.

According to Wood, Corporate Social Responsibility, also called conscience, corporate citizenship is a form of cooperate self-regulation integrated into business model (Wood, 1991). Habish, and others have also noted that approaches about CSR remain heterogeneous in most cases but can commonly be held together by corporate philanthropy (Habisch, 2005). Such cases may include monetary donations and aid given to communities and nonprofit organizations for such purposes such as education, health, environment social welfare etc. (Marquis, 2013).

Theoretical Frameworks and Global Perspective of CSR

Triple Bottom line, from its very title, depicts a pluralistic endeavor. It is a brainchild of John Elkington, who coined the term in 1994 and later used it in his book, "Cannibals with Forks: The Triple Bottom Line of 21st Century Business" where he described the social financial and environmental bottom lines. He argues that companies should prepare these bottom lines instead of focusing only on finances, thereby emphasizing the impact of a company's social, economic and environmental contract in areas of operation. The goal here should be to advance development and sustainability in business practices. (Elkington, 1997).

By using an approach, that combines people, planet and profit; businesses should be able to evaluate their performances. In the case of people, it refers to the fair practices of labor, especially to those in the communities and region where the business is operated. By the planet simply means all the practices under sustainable environmental observances. Profit here is the economic value derived after the entity deducts the cost of all inputs, including the cost of capital, (Chopra K. P, 2010).

The ways states conduct their affairs at domestic levels are not that much different from how they do with the larger comity of nations. This is backed by Liberalism orientation of international cooperation (Liberal, 1997).

One of such embracing sets of principles is the United Nations Global Compact, which is notably the largest corporate citizenship poised with objectives to adopt policies, which are socially responsible and sustainable throughout the world.

Collected from various UN conventions and declarations, ten principles were derived. The four broad areas include

Human Rights (support and respect the protection of international human rights and ensure that business observe issues of human rights abuses),

Labor Rights (ensure the freedom of association, elimination of all kind of forced and compulsory labor)

Environment (support to precautionary approaches to environmental challenges, promote environmental friendly technology)

Governance (work against corruption in all forms) (United Nations Global Compact, 2000).

The UN Guiding principles on Business and Human rights, seek to assist states and businesses commit to respecting and protecting human rights and primary freedoms in compliances with local laws. An important aspect of this is embedded in the global standards for addressing human rights violations where in the case of breach remedies are provided. This is looked at both from the static and entrepreneur levels (UNOHCHR, 2011).

The International Labor Organization (ILO) tripartite declaration of principles on multinational enterprises and social policy is another relevant international instrument to the conduct of CSR.

Labor social standards have been observed by this set of principles. Evidently, it is mainly voluntary but encourages governments, employers and multi-national organizations to work towards labor standards. It focuses on freedom of association, industrial relations employment opportunities necessary for CSR. (ILO, 2006).

Organization for Economic Cooperation and Development (OECD) guidelines also form part of the global perspectives from which CSR can be viewed.

The focus is on principles and standards of doing business responsibly in multinational corporations, mostly covering the areas of employment, human rights, environment, information disclosure, and combating bribery in all forms. The procedures for resolving disputes between corporations and communities or individuals who are adversely impacted by business activities are also embedded in these principles (OECD, 1976). This has been a tricky area.

Analysis

From China Union Investment in the Western Cluster to Putu Iron Ore in the Southeast, as well as BHP Billiton and Arcelor Mittal in the central and northern parts of Liberia, there has been concerns in multiple areas-farming, hunting, fishing and the normal livelihoods of original inhabitants. The area covers land spreading over 229,386 hectares (National Bureau of Concession Liberia Data portal). This is a substantial area which has been affected.

What is even more alarming is that, in most instances, the decision to make concessions and award contracts in the extractive industries transcends the jurisdictions of the local/host communities. This has been centered on major legal contextualization at central and or provincial level, public policies across varying structures of governments.

These are practices placed under good faith for the public good of the citizenry. However, ever since the extractive industry came to being, effects on the local communities have taken multiple dimensions ranging from environmental to basic livelihoods circumstances, which directly and indirectly affect the local population.

This becomes tremendously challenging in developing countries where low scale agriculture and subsistence farming remain as major sources of livelihoods. Therefore, the way in which companies activities affect the environment can be considered problematic, having impacts on the livelihoods of local people in multiple facets. Local people become challenged, in most cases when their homes are compromised for space to allow companies' operations. They are faced with economic difficulties and lack basic opportunities in small and medium enterprises necessary for their survival.

This has claimed the attention of a wide range of scholars including Crowther and Jatana who postulated that any actions of the organization will have an effect not just upon itself but also upon the external environment which includes both the business environment where the business resides, operates and the local societal environment (Crowther, 2008).

They further maintained that the effect of the organization may take many forms including, utilization of natural resources as part of its production processes, the enrichment of a local community through the creation of employment opportunities, transformation of the land scape due to raw material extraction or waste management. They concluded that organizations have significant impacts upon their external environment and can actually change the same through their activities.

But the alternative livelihoods which have been created by companies in the extractive industries of Liberia have proven to have limited impacts on the host communities from chain of communities in Nimba, to Cape Mount, to Grand Gedeh counties where health, education and employments are still heavily challenged.

In the view of many, including Vivian Forrester, as discussed in her book "De Terreur van de Globalisering" (the Terror of Globalization), liberalism leads to a high concentration of power of multinational entities which mostly care about their shareholders and deal ruthlessly with their employees, leaving government with little say in what mega companies do (Forrester, 2001).

Following the same path, John Cavanagh and Jerry Mander propounded that where corporate globalists see the spread and vibrant market economies, citizens movements see the power to govern being shifted away from people and communities to global financial corporations whose dedications are to short term profit making and disregard human natural concerns (Carvanagh, 2002).

The above assertions have manifest effects in Liberia, as it may be accepted giving rise to some core question like; who can be held responsible? The company's failure to uphold tasks or the government failure to monitor and ensure the commitment of firms?

Major Assumptions

Community dwellers are not extensively informed about concession areas and the benefits of the communities, thereby resulting to inherent conflict factors.

Affected areas are not managed under environmental procedures and will therefore create long term environmental circumstances.

Skills development opportunities for local staff are limited and undermines capacity development

Local authorities' role in fulfilling CRS through social development fund is politicized and does not benefit the average citizens.

Conclusion and Recommendations

The chapter mapped the basic insights of CSR and explained how the concept enhances development when performed under guided frameworks. The focus was the extractive industries in Liberia with the focus of the potential of companies in the sector to shift livelihoods of people in host communities.

A major theme was the limited significance of CSR in Liberia, thereby calling national government to increase awareness measures of the concept and ensure in Liberia that companies fulfill their requirements of CSR in support of sustainable development.

1. **Discuss some major lapses in CSR within the Liberian context- from policy formation to implementation.**

2. **What recommendations would you suggest to mitigate the lapses discussed in question one?**

3. **Are national government frameworks in place to monitor/track companies' actions and inaction in Liberia? Discuss**

4. **How can effective CRS policy formulation and implementation complement government in addressing key livelihood sectors: health, education, employment in Liberia? Explain**

Chapter 7

Tracing Vulnerabilities, Violence and Health Risks Induced by Climate Change

Introduction

The climate change literature developed over time. The debates have shifted from whether or not climate change exists to how the effects of climate change can be addressed. It has become more convincing as the earth gets hotter, increasingly causing melting of glaciers, which have resulted to high sea rise, soil intrusion, land degradation, etc.

On the other hand, it has been identified that essential interplay of these naturally related occurrences induce conflict of varying natures.

Some of these concerns are premised on the consensus that variability and change intensify the scarcity of natural resources on the African continent, where majority of the people depend on land, water and the ocean for their livelihoods- according to the African Center for Constructive Resolution of Disputes (ACCRD).

In this chapter, the natures of climate change are discussed as the nexus of conflict -from a broader perspective, to narrowed scenarios- at community levels. References are particularly placed on coastal communities along the nation's capital.

Serious health hazards, interpersonal violence and vulnerabilities because of loss of lands and forced migration due to sea erosion are analyzed with plausible assumptions and policy options recommendations as remedies.

Among the many concerns of the international system, it has been difficult placing climate change effects as a top priority.

Robin Mearns and Andrew Norton of the World Bank have variously argued that the most profound challenge facing the international community in the 21st century is climate change. They described it as much as a challenge for poverty reduction, growth and development as it is a global environmental issue (Mearns, R. and Norton, A.; 2008).

As far back in 2007, it has already been estimated by the International Panel on Climate Change (IPCC) that the world will warm between 1.8-4.2 degree Celsius within 100 years (IPCC; 2007). It also assumed that conditions of droughts, extreme precipitation, heat waves and cyclone intensity, rising sea levels, increased land degradation and changing disease prevalence would have resulted (ibid).

Elementally, these can be argued as factors of conflict at different levels. It may affect regions, communities and neighborhoods differently, depending on the potential of the climate change inducing factor(s). For example, scarcity because of forced migration or resistance to share limited facilities can result to conflict in crowded coastal communities.

(Analysis) Issues,
Plausible causes and remedial actions Vulnerabilities

Many factors position Liberia among many countries, especially Least Developing Countries (LCDs), vulnerable to impacts of climate change.

While Liberia has low carbon footprint, the effects of climate change may have severe consequences in myriad spheres. Essentially, these spheres include the sectors of agriculture, fisheries, forests, energy production related to availability of water resources, coastal areas and health.

It becomes more alarming considering the estimation that floods and sea erosion are among climate related hazards, which are likely to worsen in Liberia with assumptions of significant impact on local communities' livelihoods.

The coastal line of Liberia is susceptible to sea level rise. It is estimated that by the year 2090, Liberia will experience a sea rise of 0.13m and 0.43 as predicted by the SRESB1 (INC, 3013).

The country's coastal line itself lies on the Gulf of Guinea coastline, making it significantly exposed to Southern Atlantic annual sea storms surges that lead average tidal rises of over 2m during a brief period in early rainy season. It is a major driver of severe coastal erosion along the Montserrado Coastlines (West Point Communities, New Kru Town), Buchanan and Cestos Cities, according to the (NAPA; 2008).

The erosion lead to force migration or shorelines retreat. These scenarios have been noticed with varying distances with about 10 meters a year in higher lifted zones and about 20 meters a year in the low land along the coastal communities [Bushrod Island, Monrovia].

These stretches cover over a host of densely populated communities in Monrovia, mostly occupied by particularly poor people without adequate finances neither to employ coastal defense initiatives nor to acquire new decent lands for habitation and the conduct of livelihoods. Thus, they are compelled to live along these shores with high risks.

The effects have been far reaching and in the past forty years, a number of climate change effects have occurred, according to the Environmental Protection Agency (EPA) of Liberia.

It has been realized that factors responsible include shifting cultivation, unsustainable logging practices, unregulated coastal mining, decreasing river flows due to high evaporation, etc.

However, the National Adaption Plan that began in 2015 is the country road map that engenders evaluation of existing climate adaption and mitigation initiatives. It also includes an assessment of knowledge, capacity and implementation gaps including capacity and implementation needs. It provides a guideline for implementation of the (NAP) process in Liberia and the areas to work in short medium and long terms.

Initially, The Government of Liberia (GoL) has implemented a number of climate change related initiatives including NAP in 2008, International Communication in 2012, National Climate Change Policy and REDD+ in 2012.

The realization has been the existing lack of institutional and technical capacities on climate change adaption in Liberia that prevent the government and stakeholders from integrating fully the ACC into planning and budgeting processes and to implement adaptation strategies.

A key objective of the NAP is coastal management.

Violence

History is replete with accounts of violence in many forms. Across Africa and other parts of the world, enormous accounts point to conflict induced by climate change. Whether in the natures of communal civil violent conflicts in the north eastern area of Nigeria (Emeka E. Obioha, 2017) or the trace of the genocide in Darfur (sometime referred to as the world first conflict caused by climate change, after the conflict was sparked, at least impart, by decline in rainfall) (David Biello, 2017).

American columnist Jeffrey Sachs at an event at Columbia University in 2007 mentioned that "Don't doubt for a moment that places like Darfur are ecological disasters first and political disasters second."

Henrik Urdal in similar fashion argues that, the direst predictions about the impact of global warming warn about greatly increased risks of violent conflict over increasingly scarce resources such as freshwater and arable land (Urdal, U.;2007).

Increasingly being described as a security problem, climate change has also been viewed as a factor responsible for violent conflict. A particular aspect of vulnerability of local places and social grounds (Jon Barnett and W. Neil Adger, 2007).

A strand of this is interpersonal violence among community dwellers, which have become common in clustered communities along coastal areas in Liberia.

Health Risks

Climate change may lead to increased vulnerability to malaria, cholera and diarrhea diseases as well as increased incidences of these diseases.

Because humans have significant interactions with their environments, it follows logically that extensive relations must exist. One core area is health. The world health organization defines environment as it relates to health as "all the physical, chemical and biological factors external to a person and all related behaviors (WHO; 2006).

It has been studied that long term good health of populations depends on the continued stability and functioning of the biosphere's ecological and physical systems, often referred to as life- support system as mentioned by A.J. McMichae in "Global Climate Change and Health: an Old Story Writ Large."

Mirroring from the above, human activities along coastal areas where toilet facilities are extensively linked to water sources used for important daily uses signal serious health risks.

On another strand, malaria is very common in such areas considering the channel that both temperature and surface water have important influences on the insect vectors of vector-borne infectious disease. Of particular importance are, vector mosquito species which spread malaria and viral diseases such as dengue and yellow fever. (WHO, 2003).

Under these conditions, it can be agreed that, substantial health hazards and high risks permeate these coastal communities and seem to have no check system in place, at least not policy-wise.

Major Assumptions

The will be more effects of climate change in coastal communities unless measures are taken to ensure coastal defense; however, failure to promote awareness will cause endured exposure to climate change effects through activities like beach sand mining, dumping of harmful chemicals in sea and ocean bodies .

Interpersonal violence may increase if the trend of continuous land loss is not medicated. On the same basis, the likelihood of disease spreading among locals will remain prevalent in these clustered communities.

Conclusion and Recommendations

Climate change has been identified as a major challenge facing the planet. Along with intractable conflict across Africa, the viewpoints mentioned it as being a trigger for conflict especially with causality factors of scarcity of limited resources as in arable lands, fresh waters bodies, etc.

Some pieces of evidence were traced to the conflict prone Darfur region and parts of northern Nigeria. In coastal regions feasible for economic activities like fishing and agriculture, these triggers are more apparent.

Those susceptible to climate change include coastal communities in the Nation's Capital Monrovia, (New Kru Town, West Point etc.) as well as other cities like Buchanan in Grand Bassa and Cestos in River Cess County. With prevalence of Malaria, constant fight on occupation of new lands, mishits building closed to high sea waves, vulnerabilities, health risks interpersonal violence appear common.

It must be noted that most awareness measures have not been employed at institutional levels, nor at high schools and universities, thereby demanding the need to address such. The newly adopted National Adaption Plan must not be a mere shelve material but a tool that guides into full implementation to address climate change issues where as local actions are taken seriously in addressing this global menace being faced by Liberia and the entire comity of nations.

1. Discuss some major health risks because of Global Warming

2. Vulnerabilities expose whole societies. How does this fit in to the afro-developmental model? What considerations should policy makers consider when formulating policies?

3. Are sector agencies for climate change equipped with the technology to assess climate change risks in Liberia?

    4. How is the government addressing the issue of climate change awareness in Liberia?

About the Author

John S.M. Yormie, Jr., is an emerging Liberian Diplomat, Researcher, Lecturer and a Youth Development Personality. His interest areas include Sustainable Development, Human Security, Gender Sensitivity and Corporate Social Responsibility etc.

He earned a Master of Arts in Diplomacy Law and Business (MADLB) from the prestigious Jindal Global University in India. He holds a Post Graduate Diploma in *Diplomacy and Contemporary International Relations* from the Gabriel L. Dennis Foreign Service Institute of the Ministry of Foreign Affairs, Republic of Liberia. He earned a BA in Sociology with distinction from the Cuttington University, Suakoko Bong County, Liberia.

He is the Coordinator and Officer in Charge of Liberia's Premier Institute for Diplomatic Training; Gabriel L. Dennis Foreign Service Institute of the Ministry of Foreign Affairs. He is a Lecturer of the Political Science Department of the AME University, Liberia.

His passion of youth development positions him as the Executive Director of one of Liberia's branded NGOs, Liberia Research and Development Networks (LRDN).

He served as Lead Researcher on the recently launched news Magazine of the Liberia National Archives titled: Liberia and the United   Nations: A Long Journey of Partnership.

Known for dedication to duty, He has been acknowledged by the Minister of Foreign Affairs H.E. Gbehzohngar Milton Findley for facilitating two major protocol training, which have significantly responded to the demand of Protocol services in Liberia.

COMING SOON

An anthology on Liberia's role in major international
organizations and regional bodies.

This reader also deals with Liberia's foreign policy; how
it is formed and has changed over time. It considers
some of the factors of that change and possible trends.

www.ingramcontent.com/pod-product-compliance
Lightning Source LLC
Chambersburg PA
CBHW052100270326
41931CB00012B/2837